YOU CHOOSE

CAN YOU ESCAPE A HAUNTED BATTLEFIELD?

AN INTERACTIVE PARANORMAL ADVENTURE

BY MEGAN COOLEY PETERSON

Published by Capstone Press, an imprint of Capstone
1710 Roe Crest Drive, North Mankato, Minnesota 56003
capstonepub.com

Copyright © 2025 by Capstone. All rights reserved. No part of this publication may be reproduced in whole or in part, or stored in a retrieval system, or transmitted in any form or by any means, electronic, mechanical, photocopying, recording, or otherwise, without written permission of the publisher.

Library of Congress Cataloging-in-Publication Data is available on the Library of Congress website.

ISBN: 9781669069133 (hardcover)
ISBN: 9781669069102 (paperback)
ISBN: 9781669069119 (ebook PDF)

Summary: Readers explore haunted battlefields around the world and experience paranormal activity inspired by reports from real people.

Editorial Credits
Editor: Mandy Robbins; Designer: Dina Her; Media Researcher: Jo Miller
Production Specialist: Tori Abraham

Any additional websites and resources referenced in this book are not maintained, authorized, or sponsored by Capstone. All product and company names are trademarks™ or registered® trademarks of their respective holders.

Photo Credits
Getty Images: Evening Standard, 27, Hulton Archive, 32, Photos.com, 18, Popperfoto, 107; Library of Congress, 69, 74; NARA: Army Signal Corps Collection, 98, U.S. Coast Guard, 78; Shutterstock: JGade, 36, John Gomez, 94, Kamil Jany, 21, komkrit Preechachanwate, 67, Lagutkin Alexey, 87, mary981, 46, Morphart Creation, 16, PhotosbyAndy, 58, Raggedstone, 65, Robert Adrian Hillman, Cover, Ron Ellis, 102, Tim Weikert, 77, Triff, 8, zef art, 15

Design Elements
Shutterstock: Nik Merkulov, Olha Nion

Any additional websites and resources referenced in this book are not maintained, authorized, or sponsored by Capstone. All product and company names are trademarks™ or registered® trademarks of their respective holders.

TABLE OF CONTENTS

INTRODUCTION
ABOUT YOUR ADVENTURE 5

CHAPTER 1
A HAUNTED ASSIGNMENT 9

CHAPTER 2
THE BATTLE OF HASTINGS 17

CHAPTER 3
THE BATTLE OF GETTYSBURG 47

CHAPTER 4
THE ALLIED INVASION OF NORMANDY 79

CHAPTER 5
THE GHOSTS OF WAR 103

    MORE GHOSTLY ENCOUNTERS 106
    OTHER PATHS TO EXPLORE 108
    GLOSSARY 109
    BIBLIOGRAPHY 110
    READ MORE 111
    INTERNET SITES 111
    ABOUT THE AUTHOR 112

INTRODUCTION
ABOUT YOUR ADVENTURE

YOU work at a museum. Your boss wants you to create a new exhibit about historic battlefields. Your job is to research the history about the battles. Then you will visit the battlefields and collect stories, photographs, and objects. Rumors swirl that the battlefields are haunted. What will you do if you encounter the paranormal at a battlefield? Would you be able to complete your work, or would you run in fright?

Chapter One sets the scene. Then you choose which path to read. Follow the directions at the bottom of the page as you read the stories. The decisions you make will change your outcome. After you finish one path, go back and read the others for new perspectives and more adventures.

Turn the page to begin your adventure.

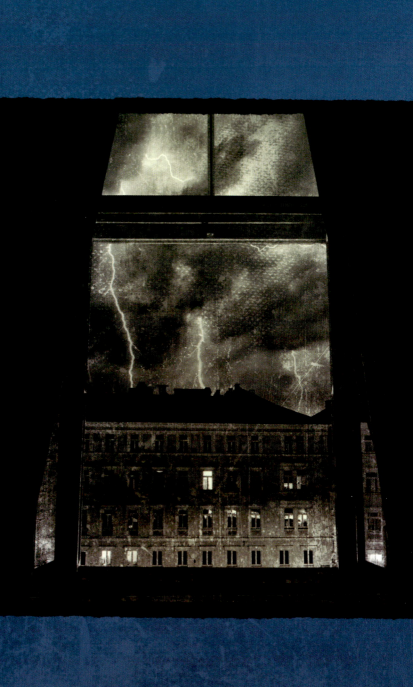

CHAPTER 1
A HAUNTED ASSIGNMENT

The wind howls outside your office window. Lightning slashes the dark sky. The room lights up as if someone just snapped a picture.

Boom! You startle, almost knocking over your coffee. Storms have always scared you, and this one promises to be a monster. You stayed late at the museum tonight to research the Battle of Gettysburg from the Civil War (1861–1865). Your boss is considering it for an exhibit.

Turn the page.

The war between the states broke out on April 12, 1861. The nation had split into two, divided on the question of slavery. Large-scale farms in southern states used enslaved workers to grow their crops. But the movement against enslavement was growing in the northern states.

In 1860, anti-slavery candidate Abraham Lincoln was elected president. White people in the South feared they would lose their labor force. Eleven southern states seceded from the United States. They formed the Confederate States of America.

As you research, you click on a website about reported hauntings at Gettysburg. You read stories of ghostly soldiers and phantom doctors performing grisly surgery. You've never had a ghostly encounter. But you're open to the possibility the stories might be true.

You pick up your coffee mug to sip some much-needed caffeine, but it's gone cold. You step out of your office and head to the staff kitchen. The museum closed hours ago, and you're the only one here. Every creak and groan sounds amplified. Another clap of thunder has your heart racing. You remind yourself it's only a storm and start brewing a fresh pot of coffee.

As you wait for the coffee to finish, the sound of footsteps startles you. They stop just outside the kitchen door. The knob turns, and the door slowly opens. Your entire body tenses.

You breathe a sigh of relief. It's your boss, Rebecca. She looks as shocked to see you as you are to see her.

"I thought I was the only one here," you say. "You scared me!"

Turn the page.

"So did I!" Rebecca says. "I've made my final decision on our next exhibit."

"The Battle of Gettysburg?" you ask, excitedly. The bloodiest battle of the Civil War took place at Gettysburg, Pennsylvania, in 1863. About 50,000 soldiers were killed or wounded there. The battlefield is now a historical park.

"Sort of," she replies. "Gettysburg might be a part of it. But this new exhibit will be something we've never done at the museum. I hope you'll take the lead on Haunted Battlefields."

You frown. "I'm sorry, did you say, 'Haunted Battlefields?' As an exhibit?"

"I want to feature battlefields with dozens of reported hauntings," Rebecca says. "And we can open in October, just in time for Halloween."

You're curious. "Which battlefields?" you ask.

"Hastings, Gettysburg, and Normandy are strong contenders," she says. "I know you'll knock Gettysburg out of the park. But how do you feel about visiting Hastings and Normandy?"

You know quite a bit about both battles. The Battle of Hastings was fought in 1066 in England. It was a fight for the English crown. During the battle, Duke William of Normandy killed King Harold of England.

William became England's new king. He also built an abbey on the spot where King Harold died, called Battle Abbey. Monks lived there for hundreds of years. You've read legends that Harold's ghost still walks the abbey grounds with an arrow lodged in his eye. Ghostly monks are also said to haunt the abbey grounds.

Turn the page.

During World War II (1939–1945), Allied forces stormed the beaches of Normandy, France. U.S., British, and Canadian troops sailed across the English Channel and landed at five beaches in Normandy.

On June 6, 1944, almost 160,000 troops converged there on what came to be called D-Day. It was a turning point in the war. The Allies liberated France from the Nazis by the end of August.

On May 8, 1945, the Germans surrendered. Reports of phantom gunfire and Nazi bunkers filled with ghosts have come out of Normandy for years.

"Are you the right person for this job?" Rebecca asks. "If the haunted stories have merit, we can borrow artifacts from other museums."

"I'd be happy to lead the Haunted Battlefields exhibit," you say. "Where do I go first?"

Rebecca smiles. "You choose!" she says just as another boom of thunder rattles the windows.

- To visit the Battle of Hastings, turn to page 17.
- To travel to Gettysburg, Pennsylvania, turn to page 47.
- To explore the beaches of Normandy, turn to page 79.

CHAPTER 2
THE BATTLE OF HASTINGS

The next morning, you book a ticket to England. On the plane, you flip through a packet of materials you printed out about the battle.

On January 5, 1066, England's King Edward died. He had no sons to take his throne. Before his death, Edward appointed Harold Godwinson as the next king. Harold worked for William as an advisor and was England's leading military general. He was also a powerful earl. Harold was crowned king on January 6.

Turn the page.

The only trouble was that King Edward had promised the throne to Duke William of Normandy years earlier. Normandy is a region in modern-day France. William was also Edward's cousin's son. When Harold Godwinson was crowned instead, William felt betrayed. He declared war against Harold. On October 14, William and his troops defeated Harold's army at the Battle of Hastings.

Harold Godwinson being shot in the eye

Construction on Battle Abbey began in 1070, four years after the battle. King William ordered the church's High Altar to be placed on the exact spot where Harold had died. Once completed, Catholic monks lived and worked at the abbey.

Today, Battle Abbey is a national park. The church is gone, and only a shell of the monks' dormitory remains. A plaque on the ground marks where Harold died. Many visitors throughout the years have reported monks walking all over the park. Yet the staff says no monks work there. Some people believe the monks are ghosts. But you wonder if there's another explanation.

You read stories about how King Harold's ghost wanders the grounds with an arrow stuck in his eye. Other stories tell of a ghostly woman in a red dress and blood in the fields. You wonder if they're true.

Turn the page.

The plane lands, and the weather is cool and gray. You rent a car and drive through the English countryside. Finally, you arrive in the small town of Battle in Sussex County. As you drive along the high street, you're charmed by the quaint buildings. You can't imagine a bloody battle taking place here.

Up ahead, the gatehouse to Battle Abbey rises above the roofs. The gatehouse was added in the 1300s. It served as the abbey's main entrance for staff, traders, and merchants.

As you enter the grounds, you think about the men who died here. About 6,000 soldiers from England and Normandy lost their lives during the Battle of Hastings.

The back of your neck prickles, like you're being watched. But when you turn around, no one's there.

Tourists mill about, reading historical signs and following tour guides. You could go into the visitor center. There are artifacts and tour guides inside. Or you could explore the abbey grounds on your own.

The gatehouse at Battle Abbey

- To go to the visitor center museum, turn to page 22.
- To explore the grounds on your own, turn to page 25.

As you head toward the visitor center, a woman in a flowing red gown passes in front of you. She enters through the open door. Her dress looks like it's from the Middle Ages. It has flowing sleeves and is gathered around the waist. Is she a reenactor? No one else is dressed like that. Curious, you hurry in through the door. But once you're inside, she's nowhere to be seen.

You join a tour group. The guide has a deep, booming voice. "Pope Alexander II supported Duke William's claim to the throne," the guide says. "After the battle, the Pope wanted the new king to honor the dead. In response, William built the abbey. Historians guess 6,000 died here. That might explain all the alleged ghost sightings."

Your ears perk up. This is just the kind of information Rebecca wants to include at the museum. You're glad you decided to take a tour.

The guide leads the group to a large wall display. "This is a replica of the Bayeux Tapestry. It was embroidered with wool thread around the time of the battle. It shows the Norman conquest of England, including the Battle of Hastings."

Tourists move closer to the wall for a better look. You study a section that shows King Harold's dragon banner. It was shaped like a windsock. A breeze would have inflated the banner, making it appear to fly. During the Middle Ages, armies used banners to mark positions on the battlefield. Some soldiers, called standard bearers, carried large banners. Knights attached smaller banners to their lances.

You catch the tour guide's attention. "Was Harold's dragon banner ever found?" you ask. You hope this museum might even loan it to your museum for display.

Turn the page.

The guide shakes his head. "I'm afraid not. But that would have been an amazing find!"

The guide leads the group to a case that displays a medieval dice and game piece. "Monks attended several church services each day," the guide says. "They spent hours reading, praying, and taking care of the grounds. Games helped them relax."

As you move to the next case, the temperature drops. You look around for an open window, but there are no windows. Goose bumps break out on your arms. You see a flash of red go into the next room. It's the woman you saw earlier.

- To follow the woman, turn to page 27.
- To keep listening to the tour guide, turn to page 31.

You walk among the ruins of Battle Abbey. In the 1500s, most of the original abbey buildings were taken down. The stones were given away, including those used to build the abbey church. Other buildings, such as the monk's dormitory and the gatehouse still stand.

Moving onto the abbey's terrace, you overlook the rolling hills where the battle took place. Battle Abbey sits on Senlac Hill, where Harold's troops were stationed. From this hill, his men could see William's troops a mile south on Telham Hill.

William's troops had sailed to England two weeks before the battle. They were well rested and ready to fight. Harold's men, however, had just battled at Stamford Bridge on September 25. When Harold learned William was in England, he gathered extra troops and hurried to Hastings.

Turn the page.

To begin the battle, William's archers set out first. They moved across the valley toward the English troops. Harold's finest soldiers, called housecarls, hid behind a shield wall. They dodged the Norman archers, who had to shoot their arrows uphill. William's men retreated. But the battle was far from over.

As you recall the events of the battle, a church bell starts ringing. Startled, you look around for a bell tower but can't find one. In the Middle Ages, armies waited for church bells to begin fighting. You check your watch. It's 9:00 a.m., which is when historians think the Battle of Hastings began.

- To follow the bell sound, turn to page 29.
- To head inside the visitor center, turn to page 31.

You leave the tour group to follow the woman in red. She's not in the next room or the next. Outside, you scan the area, but you don't see her.

Disappointed, you see a sign about the battle. It says the abbey was built on Senlac Hill, where King Harold's troops gathered for battle. They could see William's troops a mile south on Telham Hill. Norman troops marched through the valley toward Senlac Hill. Their first assault on the English failed. The Normans pulled back.

The site of the Battle of Hastings

Turn the page.

Something red flickers near a large oak tree. It's the woman you saw earlier! You're determined to talk to her this time. Perhaps she's a cosplayer. She might be a great source of information. But as you draw closer, you notice her feet aren't quite touching the ground. And she's flickering like a candle's flame. You can see right through her.

You read that King Harold's wife, Edith Swan-neck, was at the battle. According to legend, Edith waited by an oak tree as the soldiers fought. She later identified Harold's body on the battlefield. Have you just encountered the ghost of Edith Swan-neck?

- To approach the ghost, turn to page 37.
- To rejoin the tour, turn to page 31.

The ringing bell grows louder the closer you get to the monks' dormitory. But as soon as you reach the dorm, the ringing stops.

That's odd, you think. You decide there must be a church nearby.

You shake your head and explore what's left of the dormitory. The monks would have slept in this room. You close your eyes and imagine beds lining the walls and a fire roaring in the hearth. You can almost see the robed monks going about their daily life.

When you open your eyes, you are shocked to see a man in a long black robe scurrying through the dorm ruins. He wears a sash tied around his waist. His gray hair is cut very short. The monks who lived here wore robes. Is he a reenactor?

Turn the page.

Curiosity gets the better of you, and you follow him out of the dormitory and around a corner. But he's disappeared. You feel a little nervous and confused. Where could he have gone?

You notice a door that leads underneath the dorm and decide to check it out. Maybe that's where the man went.

- Turn to page 35.

The tour moves into a room housing replicas of medieval weapons. The guide holds a long, tapering sword. The blade is double-edged. A groove down the blade's center makes it lighter and easier to swing.

"The sword was the most popular weapon of the time," he explains. "Swords were passed down from generation to generation. They were even given names, such as 'brand flame' and 'battle-friend.'"

The next display features other weapons used at the battle, such as spears, maces, and bows and arrows. "Duke William brought many more archers to the battle than King Harold," the guide explains. "His knights also rode on horseback. Harold's men used their horses for travel, but not during fighting."

Turn the page.

The tour group follows the guide outside. The abbey church was taken down in the 1500s. A plaque on the ground marks the High Alter where King Harold was killed.

"The Bayeux Tapestry shows King Harold shot through the eye with an arrow," the guide says. "I've heard rumors of a ghostly knight spotted at the abbey. He has an arrow lodged in his eye."

A scene from the Bayeux Tapestry

As the rest of the group talks excitedly about King Harold's ghost, you move closer to the plaque. It's wet, likely from rain. But it looks dark, almost . . . like blood. You're about to reach down and touch it when something silver flashes nearby.

A figure dressed in armor hobbles down a path. It might be a reenactor. But this figure is completely silent. You don't even hear footsteps on the pebbled ground.

Soon, the tour guide signals for everyone to follow. He wants to take you to the Common Room, a room under the dormitory where the monks relaxed.

- To follow the figure, turn to page 34.
- To go to the Common Room, turn to page 35.

You break off from the tour group and follow the figure. If the abbey is putting on a reenactment, where are all the other actors? You have an uneasy feeling about this.

The figure suddenly vanishes. You turn in a circle, frantically looking for the knight. But he's nowhere to be found. You're about to rejoin the tour when the figure reappears at the High Altar plaque. His body flickers and fades. Is there something wrong with your vision? You rub your eyes. That's when you notice a long arrow lodged in one of the man's eyes. Blood runs down his face.

It's not a reenactor at all, but the ghost of King Harold himself! Suddenly, he locks eyes with you.

- To run away into the field, turn to page 39.
- To approach King Harold's ghost, turn to page 41.

The Common Room lies below the monks' dormitory. The air grows colder as you descend the old stone steps. Arched stone ceilings soar overhead. Several tour groups move about the space.

"The monks used this room to relax in," one of the tour guides explains. "After a long day, they might have played games or discussed ideas. And of course, some say the monks never left."

"Like, ghosts?" a visitor asks.

The guide smiles. "That's the rumor."

As the tour groups file out of the Common Room, you notice a man in a white robe. He stands by himself in a corner. He looks like a monk. As you approach him, he glides away. His movements seem unnatural.

Turn the page.

The smell of something rotten wafts over you. A pile of rotting apples sits on the floor where the monk just stood. Your heart beats faster. The apples weren't there when you first arrived. Should you follow the monk or head to the visitor center? Maybe someone there can give you some answers.

- To follow the monk, turn to page 42.
- To go to the visitor center, turn to page 44.

On wobbly legs, you slowly approach the ghost. The spirit grows fainter the closer you get.

"Are you Edith Swan-neck?" you ask in a shaking voice. "Are you looking for Harold?"

The ghost doesn't speak or move. You're afraid she will disappear altogether. There's something about this ghost that makes you sad. She seems lost. Maybe you can help her. "I know where Harold is," you say. "I can lead you to him."

You point to where the High Altar once stood. The ghost blooms back into color. You walk toward the spot where King Harold died. You wonder if the ghost is following you, but you're too afraid to look back.

A large stone plaque has been set into the ground where Harold fell. You slowly turn around, but the ghost in red is gone.

Turn the page.

The air suddenly grows icy cold. A shape begins to form in front of you. At first, you think it's the woman in red. But then the shape becomes a man in full body armor. An arrow sticks out of his eye. Blood runs down his face. It's King Harold Godwinson! You scramble backward and trip over something, smacking your head on the ground. Everything goes black.

You wake up in a local hospital with a pounding headache. Your trip to Battle Abbey has been cut short. But your memories will haunt you forever.

THE END

To follow another path, turn to page 15.
To learn more about ghosts of war, turn to page 103.

You stumble into the open field, relieved to have escaped Harold's ghost. But your relief doesn't last long. Blood oozes up from the grass. Trumpets blast, even though there are no musicians. The clang of swords and screams of battle surround you.

Suddenly, you're in the battle itself. Swords clash. Arrows whiz through the air, narrowly missing your head. You want to run, but there are soldiers everywhere. They don't seem to see you. Soon, you hear rumblings that Duke William has died in battle.

"Is it true?" a Norman soldier asks. "Has our William lost his life?"

The other Norman soldiers seem confused. A man on a black horse rides to where you stand. He rips off his helmet. It's Duke William!

Turn the page.

"I am still alive, and with God's help, I shall win!"

A cheer breaks out among the Norman soldiers. A knight gallops toward you on his horse, his sword at the ready. You close your eyes, too terrified to move.

When your eyes open, you're in a cold sweat on the ground. There's no one else on the field. Was it all a dream? You don't wait around to find out. Someone else will have to finish the research for the haunted battlefields exhibit.

THE END

To follow another path, turn to page 15.
To learn more about ghosts of war, turn to page 103.

You stand before King Harold Godwinson of England. The arrow lodged in his eye looks painful. Blood covers his face. As the sunlight hits him, he fades in and out. You're too afraid to move or utter a single word.

Suddenly, a breeze whips up, and Harold's ghost fades away. You reach for where he just stood. The air is like ice.

As you turn to leave, you notice a slight bulge in the gravel. You drop to your knees and start pushing away the rocks. You unearth a small bit of fabric. It's a dark rust color. After more careful digging, you pull out a crumpled, dirty red flag. It has a dragon sewn on it. Could this have been King Harold's battle flag?

THE END

To follow another path, turn to page 15.
To learn more about ghosts of war, turn to page 103.

There are many chambers under the dormitory. Perhaps the monk went into one of them. These rooms may have been used to store food and other goods. You search each one of them, but they're all empty.

Finally, you enter a storage area called the undercroft. It's also empty. Still, you feel a presence, as if someone is with you.

"Hello?" you say. "Is anyone down here?" You are met with silence. Feeling unsettled, you leave the room and close the wooden door behind you.

Suddenly, there's a banging from the other side of the door. You jump in surprise and fear.

"Help! Let me out!" a man cries.

The undercroft was empty a moment ago. How can this be?

You quickly whip open the door. The room is still empty, just as you left it. You slam the door and hurry to your car. No living person could have possibly been crying out from in there.

You're ready to leave the ghosts of Battle Abbey behind. You hope Rebecca won't be too disappointed in you.

THE END

To follow another path, turn to page 15.
To learn more about ghosts of war, turn to page 103.

Your heart is still racing when you enter the visitor center. A man at the front desk gives you a strange look.

"Can I help you?" he asks.

You lean against the counter. Your hands shake. "Um, yes," you begin. "There was a man in the Common Room dressed like a monk. Are there any performers here today?"

The worker chuckles, though you don't find it funny. "Don't mean to laugh, mate. But you're not the first visitor to rub elbows with one of our dearly departed monks."

You swallow. "You mean . . . I saw a ghost?"

He nods. "Quite a few phantom monks still lurk about the abbey grounds. Some wear black robes, others brown, or even white. I've seen one myself walking near the old dorm."

"What about the apples?" you ask, your voice shaking. "There was a whole pile rotting in the Common Room."

"The ghostly apples, you mean," he says. "The monks probably stored some food in the Common Room."

Ghostly apples? That doesn't make any sense. You hurry back to the Common Room to see them again. But when you arrive, the apples have vanished.

THE END

To follow another path, turn to page 15.
To learn more about ghosts of war, turn to page 103.

A statue of Jennie Wade stands outside her former home.

CHAPTER 3
THE BATTLE OF GETTYSBURG

On your drive to Gettysburg, you listen to a podcast about the so-called hauntings at the battlefield.

The story of the Jennie Wade house sends chills up your spine. Jennie was hit by a stray bullet while baking bread. She was the only civilian death at Gettysburg. Visitors to the house say the spirits of Jennie and several children remain. You shiver as you arrive at the Gettysburg National Military Park.

Turn the page.

On July 1, 1863, the Union and Confederate armies clashed on these grounds. Around 165,000 soldiers fought for three days. Fighting ended on July 3. Around 50,000 men were wounded or dead.

General George Meade, the Union leader, won the battle. The Confederate Army, led by General Robert E. Lee, retreated south. The Battle of Gettysburg was the turning point of the Civil War. But it would be another two years before the Confederates surrendered.

You spend the morning listening to tour guides, taking photos, and watching reenactments. As you finish a picnic lunch, a woman at the next table is fiddling with her camera. She accidentally knocks her bag to the ground. Several objects spill onto the grass, and you help her pick them up.

You hand her a small electronic device. "What's this used for?" you ask. It looks like a radio.

"This is a spirit box," she explains, turning it over in her hands. "It uses radio waves to communicate with spirits. I'm here doing research for a book I'm writing about the ghosts of Gettysburg."

You explain that you're working on a haunted battlefields exhibit. "I'm not sure I even believe in ghosts," you admit. "But I'm trying to keep an open mind."

She stands and gathers her equipment. "I'm heading over to Iverson's Pits. I've heard it's teeming with ghosts." She tells you her name is Rita and invites you to tag along.

Turn the page.

Iverson's Pits was the sight of a failed attack by Confederate General Alfred Iverson. You could follow the ghost hunter there. Or you could go to the Angle, a famous piece of stone wall. Soldiers clashed there during Pickett's Charge, the final battle at Gettysburg.

- To go to Iverson's Pits with Rita, go to the next page.
- To continue on your own to the Angle, turn to page 54.

The walk to Iverson's Pits isn't far. Soon, you arrive in an open, grassy area. You tell Rita a little bit about the battle.

"On July 1, Confederate Brigadier General Alfred Iverson led a North Carolina brigade. They marched across that flat, open field toward a line of trees on Oak Ridge," you say, pointing.

"Iverson believed they would surprise Union troops stationed there. But he didn't know there were Union soldiers hiding behind a stone wall in the field. As his men approached, Union troops popped up from behind the wall and fired."

"Many of the Confederates were killed there," you continue. "They were buried in hastily dug pits. That's why this area is called Iverson's Pits."

Rita nods. She is fascinated by the details.

Turn the page.

"That would explain why some of the first ghostly sightings at Gettysburg were reported here at Iverson's Pits," she says.

Rita digs around in her bag and pulls out another device. "This is my EMF meter," she says. "It can pick up changes in the electromagnetic field. Big changes might mean a ghost is nearby."

You hold your breath as she turns on the EMF meter. She moves in a slow circle, holding the machine in front of her. Soon, lights on the device flash rapidly.

"I see something!" Rita says. You look where she's pointing. "See those white orbs?"

You squint. Sure enough, faint specks of light float near the ground in the distance.

"Yes. What are they?" you ask.

"Orbs are spirits in the form of tiny balls of light," she explains. "Orbs often show up in photographs and on video. Sometimes, you can even see them in person."

You're about to follow the orbs when you notice a fine white mist slowly advancing over the stone wall nearby.

That's odd, you think. *There isn't a cloud in the sky or mist anywhere else.*

- To follow the white orbs, turn to page 57.
- To investigate the mist at the stone wall, turn to page 58.

You head to the Angle on Cemetery Ridge. On July 3, General Robert E. Lee decided to attack the Union there. This attack was later named Pickett's Charge.

Before the charge, Confederate artillery fired at the middle of the Union line for two hours. Many shells exploded too early or not at all. Some landed behind the Union line.

The artillery fire had failed. But Lee didn't know that. He believed the Union's middle was now its weakest point.

At about 3:00 p.m., Pickett's Charge began. Between 12,000 and 15,000 Confederate troops marched from Seminary Ridge to Cemetery Ridge. They had to cross a mile of open farmland.

The Union troops had the advantage of the high ground. They killed, wounded, or captured around 6,500 Confederate soldiers.

You arrive at a jutting piece of stone wall known as the Angle. This was supposed to be the Confederate's main attack spot that day. But only around 100 Confederates made it over the wall. Lee's army never advanced farther north than this stone wall.

You turn to face Culp's Hill to the northeast. The Confederates had attacked the Union there the day before Pickett's Charge.

Suddenly, you hear what sounds like shouting and musket fire coming from the hill. Perhaps there's a reenactment going on. You check the schedule of events on your phone. Nothing is scheduled for Culp's Hill.

Turn the page.

As you amble toward the hill, you spot a man dressed in a white doctor's coat standing near the Codori farmhouse. This farm saw lots of fighting and death during Pickett's Charge. The farmhouse even became a field hospital.

The man might be a reenactor. He could tell you more about what is going on at Culp's Hill. Or maybe you should check it out yourself.

- To head to Culp's Hill, turn to page 61.
- To follow the doctor to the Codori farmhouse, turn to page 62.

At this point, you're already stuck on the orbs. You and Rita slowly approach them. The temperature drops, and the hairs on your arms stand up.

The orbs grow larger and more solid. They hover just above the ground. You wonder if they will grow and take the shape of spirits. But when Rita takes a photograph, they vanish. You sigh in disappointment.

"Orbs disappear all the time," she says. "Sometimes, the spirits aren't ready to communicate. It's still a cool encounter, though." She pulls out her notebook and starts writing.

You remember the strange mist you saw earlier. Together, you and Rita return to the stone wall.

At the wall, the mist has grown even thicker. It looks as if ghostly white fingers are clawing at the rough stones. You shiver.

As you walk along, you stumble over a rock sticking out of the ground. You drop down and see that it's not a rock at all. It's a cannonball! It is perfectly round with a hole where the fuse would have been.

"I found something!" you call out Rita. She rushes over to you. "It's a cannonball," you explain.

"Where?" she asks.

When you look back at the ground, the cannonball's not there. You wish you had picked it up. You frantically search the area. But all you find is an impression left in the grass.

"I swear it was right there," you say.

"A phantom cannonball," Rita remarks. "That's a new one!"

Cannonballs don't just disappear into thin air. You consider finding a park ranger to ask about it. But then you notice a man at the other end of the wall. He's dressed in a ratty blue Union uniform and carries a musket. He must have been part of the reenactment you watched earlier. He might know something about the disappearing cannonball.

Turn the page.

As you step toward him, Rita taps your shoulder. Her eyes are huge as she points to the center of the field. Hundreds of white handkerchiefs flutter above the ground, as if held by unseen hands. During the battle, some of Iverson's soldiers waved them to show surrender.

You rub your eyes, but they're still there. Have Iverson's men returned from beyond the grave?

- To approach the apparent reenactor, turn to page 64.
- To investigate the handkerchiefs, turn to page 66.

Up ahead is the Observation Tower on Culp's Hill. You're sure it has great views of the entire battlefield. Then you'll know what's going on, and you can take some photos for the museum.

As you head to the tower, orange light flickers through some trees. It's a campfire burning near a large boulder. Campfires aren't allowed at Gettysburg.

A blast of wind swirls around the hill, rustling leaves and blowing up debris. But the flames don't move at all.

- To investigate the fire, turn to page 68.
- To climb the Observation Tower on Culp's Hill, turn to page 70.

During Pickett's Charge, thousands of Confederates marched through Codori farmland. The farmhouse and barn were used as field hospitals. Doctors scrambled to help as many people as they could. Piles of amputated limbs were a common sight.

Hundreds of dead soldiers were buried on Codori land, as well as on other farm sites. For years after the battle, farm workers around Gettysburg ploughed up bones of dead soldiers.

As you near the brick farmhouse, the man in the white coat disappears around the side of the house. He almost seems to float. But that can't be possible, can it? You follow him, but he seems to have disappeared.

You remember the podcast you listened to on the way here. It talked about ghostly doctors and soldiers reported at Pennsylvania Hall at Gettysburg College. The hall was a makeshift hospital during the battle too. You should talk to their staff about any ghostly experiences they may have had. After all, fighting at Gettysburg wasn't limited to farm fields. The town itself was part of the battlefield too.

As you turn to leave, movement in the Codori house catches your eye. A shadowy figure flutters behind a curtain. You get a strange feeling in the pit of your stomach. Is that where the man went?

- To go to Pennsylvania Hall, turn to page 72.
- To investigate the shadowy figure, turn to page 75.

You leave Rita and approach the reenactor. The mist begins to spread out from the wall, blanketing the grass in white. The man turns and walks into the mist, away from you.

"Hello?" you call out as you follow. "Sir?"

But he doesn't stop. The mist now covers your feet and ankles. Up ahead, the man dims as he enters a thicket of trees. His body is almost see-through. It must be shadows playing tricks on you. But then, the mist and the man both vanish!

Suddenly, the sounds of gunfire pierce the silence. You whip around, looking for the source. But there are no reenactors here, just the green grasses and rolling hills of Gettysburg. The sounds of fighting fade away, replaced by birdsong. You question the eerie experience for the rest of your life.

THE END

To follow another path, turn to page 15.

To learn more about ghosts of war, turn to page 103.

You and Rita hurry toward the waving handkerchiefs. The closer you get, the more tattered they become. A few even have blood on them. You realize some of Iverson's men might still be lying in the ground below. Maybe you shouldn't disturb their final resting place.

You're about to turn back when the handkerchiefs become daisies swaying in the breeze. You were certain they were bloody fabric only a moment ago.

Rita laughs nervously. "I knew this place was haunted, but this is incredible!" She starts snapping photos of the flowers.

After saying goodbye to Rita, you walk the fields alone. Just a few days ago, you didn't believe in ghosts. Now you can't wait to tell Rebecca about your experiences here. This battlefield is perfect for the exhibit.

Now you can contact other museums and historians. They might loan your museum some artifacts.

You feel a sneeze coming on and reach into your pocket for a tissue. Instead, you pull out a tattered white handkerchief. Your whole body goes cold. The last thing you see before you pass out are the dancing daisies.

THE END

To follow another path, turn to page 15.
To learn more about ghosts of war, turn to page 103.

A wildfire would damage these historic woods. You run to try to put it out quickly. But when you arrive at the boulder, the fire is gone. There are no scorch marks. No ashes or charred wood remain. Was it only a trick of the light?

At the bottom of the hill, you find a park ranger. "I saw a fire burning on Culp's Hill," you tell her, pointing behind you. "But now I can't find it."

The ranger's face goes pale. "I've seen fires on that hill," she says, a faraway look in her eyes. "But when I investigate them, they vanish. These disappearing fires burn in other parts of Gettysburg too."

"What do you think they are?" you ask.

"I don't know. The soldiers who fought here would have started fires at night," she says.

Shivering, you look back at Culp's Hill. There are no traces of fire now. But the ghostly flames you encountered at Gettysburg have been burned into your memory.

Civil War fighting on Culp's Hill

THE END

To follow another path, turn to page 15.
To learn more about ghosts of war, turn to page 103.

After climbing seven flights of stairs, you arrive at the top of Culp's Hill Observation Tower. No one else is there. You're out of breath as you look out over Gettysburg. From here, you can see battlefield landmarks like Big and Little Round Top and Cemetery Ridge.

The sound of footsteps on the stairs startles you. Someone must be coming up. But the footsteps stop just below the platform. You hold your breath, waiting for another person to appear.

Finally, you peer down the staircase. It's empty. You look over the edge of the platform. There's no one on the ground below. The park is quiet. Are you the only one left?

The footsteps return, louder than before. Sweat breaks out on your back. Your heart pounds in your chest.

"Hello?" you say. "Is anyone there?" No one answers. As soon as you move to the stairs, the footsteps stop. The stairs remain empty.

You quickly climb down the empty tower stairs. Once you're on the ground, you search the area near the tower. But there are no other tourists here. Your whole body turns cold when you realize a ghost must have made those footsteps.

THE END

To follow another path, turn to page 15.
To learn more about ghosts of war, turn to page 103.

The drive to Pennsylvania Hall takes only a few minutes. You park before a tall brick building with white columns. Built in 1837, the hall was a dormitory. Today, it's office space for the college.

You go to the front desk and explain that you're researching haunted battlefields. You ask about the alleged hauntings at Pennsylvania Hall.

The woman at the desk shudders. "I went down to the basement one night to get some office supplies," she says. "I heard a man cry out in pain."

"Could I go down there?" you ask. It's the last place you want to go. But if you want your exhibit to be successful, you don't have a choice.

"Be my guest," she says. "But I'm not going with you."

As the elevator begins its descent, your stomach lurches. When it stops at the basement level, you change your mind and jam the button for the main floor. But nothing happens. Then the doors open, and the scene before you makes you sick.

A Civil War surgeon stands at a table with crude-looking surgical instruments. Blood soils his once-white coat. Soldiers sit slumped against the walls. Some are bleeding and others bandaged. You push more buttons, but the elevator stays put. The doors won't close.

A soldier lies groaning on the table. His leg is mangled. The surgeon picks up a bloody scalpel. He starts cutting into the skin. Suddenly, everything around you goes black.

Turn the page.

You wake up on the elevator floor. The doctors and wounded soldiers have vanished. But the scene has been burned into your memory. From that day on, you see the wounded soldier every night when you close your eyes.

Pennsylvania Hall

THE END

To follow another path, turn to page 15.
To learn more about ghosts of war, turn to page 103.

Peering into the dark window, you see nothing. *It must have been my imagination*, you tell yourself. You turn to leave when something creaks behind you. You spin around as the front door slowly opens. You want to run, but your feet feel rooted in place.

A park ranger steps outside, and you breathe a sigh of relief. "I thought I saw a shape or a shadow inside. I didn't realize anyone was here," you tell the ranger. "Gettysburg has me a little spooked."

The ranger smiles and joins you in the yard. "It spooks me a little bit too."

"How do you mean?" you ask.

He nods back at the house. "I live here with my family. I often hear footsteps when I'm the only one home."

Turn the page.

"I saw someone earlier," you say, hoping he'll believe you. "A man wearing a doctor's coat. Does the park host any medical reenactments?"

The ranger shakes his head. "None that I'm aware of," he says. "But I believe Gettysburg is a truly haunted battlefield."

"I think you may be right," you say. The ghosts of Gettysburg will stick with you long after you leave this haunted place.

THE END

To follow another path, turn to page 15.
To learn more about ghosts of war, turn to page 103.

The D-Day Invasion of Normandy

CHAPTER 4
THE ALLIED INVASION OF NORMANDY

Your plane touches down in Normandy, France. You rent a car and drive along the coast. Soon, you arrive in the small seaside village of Vierville-sur-Mer. The weather is warm and breezy. Seagulls squawk overhead, and waves roll gently onto the sand. You'll have plenty of time to go sightseeing later. Now you need to remember your research on World War II.

Turn the page.

The war began in 1939 when Germany invaded Poland. Adolf Hitler and the Nazi Party wanted to expand Germany's power and borders. Germany, along with Italy and Japan, formed the Axis Powers. The Allied Powers of France, Great Britain, Canada, China, the United States, and the Soviet Union fought against them. By 1944, the Axis Powers controlled most of Europe. The Allies needed a way into Europe. They decided to invade at Normandy, France.

Early on the morning of June 6, 1944, Allied forces launched a massive water attack on the beaches of Normandy. This attack was called D-Day. Hitler had set up defenses along the coast of France. The Germans built bunkers into the cliffs above the beaches. From the bunkers, they could gun down approaching ships and ground troops.

U.S. Army Rangers attacked a German bunker at Pointe Du Hoc. This 100-foot-high cliff sits west of Omaha beach. At the same time, paratroopers landed behind enemy lines. They secured some bridges and roads and blew up others to stop German tanks. They disarmed large guns aimed at Allied ships and troops.

Allied ground troops landed at five beaches. The beaches had the code names Gold, Juno, Sword, Utah, and Omaha. Many soldiers lost their lives on those beaches that morning.

You park near your hotel and check in. "*Bonjour*," the clerk greets you as he hands you a key to your room. "What brings you here?"

"I'm researching the Allied invasion on D-Day," you explain. "And the stories of ghostly sightings that followed."

Turn the page.

The clerk nods. "You'll find no shortage of ghost stories on our beaches," he says. "I've seen strange shadows down near the water. My cousin heard phantom gunfire once. And more than a few tourists have gotten spooked up at the old bunkers."

- To walk along Omaha beach where many Allied troops landed, go to the next page.
- To explore the German observation bunker at Pointe Du Hoc, turn to page 84.

You walk along the sand of Omaha Beach. It's a sunny day, without a cloud in the sky. The weather on D-Day, however, was overcast. That morning, the Allies launched the largest fleet in history. Almost 5,000 landing ships and assault crafts crossed the English Channel. They were protected by dozens of battleships, cruisers, destroyers, and escort ships. Ahead of them, minesweepers cleared the water of German mines.

As you gaze out at the ocean, a spec appears on the horizon. A ship slowly comes into view. The ship is long and gray with smokestacks. It almost looks like a military ship. You blink, and it disappears as quickly as you saw it. *Ghost ships aren't real*, you tell yourself. The hotel clerk's stories about ghosts must have spooked you. Plus, you're tired from your flight. A nap might help.

- To keep walking along the beach, turn to page 88.
- To return to your hotel and take a nap, turn to page 98.

The observation bunker at Pointe Du Hoc served as a command center for the Germans. Made of reinforced concrete, the bunker held nine soldiers. It had a handful of rooms, including a radio room, a telephone room, and a map room. The observation room overlooked the cliff. Soldiers could watch the English Channel through a slit in the concrete.

You walk down the steps toward the entrance. A tour group stands next to an opening set in the outer wall. It looks like a small window filled with metal instead of glass. And there's a small hole in the center of the metal. The tour guide gestures at the opening.

"A German machine gunner stood in a small room on the other side of this opening. He aimed through this small hole," he says. "Notice how rough the metal is? When Army Rangers stormed this bunker, their grenades damaged it."

A few tourists are whispering about the bunker being haunted. You try to listen more closely, but they leave the bunker.

The air grows quiet as you head past a metal gate and into the bunker. You turn left through the main inner door and continue to the empty bunk room. From your research, you know the men slept and played games here. The bunks are gone, but you can see where they hooked onto the wall.

An odd sensation creeps along the back of your neck, like someone's behind you. But you're the only one in the room.

"Hello?" you say. Your voice is swallowed up in the tomb-like space. You're not sure you want to stay in here.

- To move on to the map room, turn to page 86.
- To explore outside of the bunker, turn to page 90.

Your footsteps echo as you walk into the map room. During the war, there would have been a large table covered with maps. Officers would have plotted out targets and sent orders to fire the large guns.

You blink, and something changes. Suddenly, the room is filled with people—or spirits of people. Ghostly German officers bustle about the room. They wear gray military jackets with the eagle and swastika insignia. Some read maps, while others call out orders in German.

A phone rings in the telephone room just off the map room. A German officer says something to you. He points to the telephone room. Does he want you to answer it? This can't be real, can it?

- To answer the call, turn to page 95.
- To run out of the bunker, turn to page 90.

A field telephone used by the German Army during World War II

You're bound to see something of interest if you keep walking. Sure enough, the ruins of Mulberry Harbor eventually appear in the distance. With no ports to land at, Allied forces built two artificial harbors at Normandy. These harbors calmed the rough ocean waters so Allied craft could land safely. Inside the harbor, boats docked at temporary piers. Floating roads connected the piers to the beach.

Out of nowhere, fog overtakes the beach. The sky was blue just a moment ago. Now you can't see more than a foot in front of you. But you hear plenty. The sound of planes roaring overhead makes your heart gallop. Something zings past your ear, and you dive for the sand. You cover your head with your arms. Bombs blast around you. None of this can be real, you tell yourself. But where are these sounds coming from?

Suddenly, the fog lifts. The sounds of war fade away. The beach is clear again, the sky a friendly blue. A family having a picnic nearby laughs as they eat. They obviously didn't hear a thing.

You stumble down the beach with your legs feeling like jelly. You notice a trail of something dark in the sand. Is it blood? Turning in a circle, you don't see any injured people. Still, the bloody trail unnerves you.

- To continue to the Mulberry Harbor ruins, turn to page 91.
- To follow the trail, turn to page 93.

In a panic, you run out of the bunker. You climb onto the top of it and look out over the cliff. Water crashes into the rocks below. It's a 100-foot drop from here to the sea. At around 7:00 a.m. on D-Day, Rangers began climbing the steep cliff face. They used rope ladders to scale the stone. Above them, Germans tossed grenades and fired at them. Allied ships gave the Rangers cover as they climbed.

You're about ready to go back to your hotel, but you peer over the edge one more time. You're surprised to see a man climbing the cliff face! He's dressed in some type of brown uniform and wears a helmet. The wind starts gusting. What if the man falls? Does he need help?

- To try to help the man, turn to page 96.
- To go back to your hotel, turn to page 98.

You arrive at the ruins of Mulberry Harbor. A concrete block the size of a small building rests in the sand. As you examine the ruins, you hear a voice say, "Help me! My leg! Help!"

You scurry around the ruins, desperate to find whoever is hurt. But there's no one else around.

You're about to leave when the faint outline of a man appears next to the ruins. He wears a U.S. military uniform. And he's missing a leg.

The soldier takes a drink from a canteen wrapped in canvas. He locks eyes with you. Opening your mouth, you try to speak. But your voice won't work. Soon, he fades away.

Turn the page.

There, at the base of the ruins, something sticks out of the sand. You drop down and dig it out. It's a canteen wrapped in tattered canvas. The faded stamp of "U.S." is barely visible.

You can only hope the soldier with the missing leg got the help he needed. His cries for help will echo in your mind for many years to come.

THE END

To follow another path, turn to page 15.
To learn more about ghosts of war, turn to page 103.

You follow the dark trail as it snakes along the sand. It stops and starts, disappearing for stretches at a time.

Suddenly, you hear someone yelling an order in German. You look around, but there's no one there. The shouting stops. When you face forward, you're on a different beach now—Sword Beach. It's miles from Omaha Beach. And you haven't been walking that long. How did you get here? You look down at the sand and feel a lump in your throat. The bloody trail is still there.

Goose bumps bloom down your back as you walk on. Finally, the trail stops at a small monument. It honors the Allied paratroopers that landed at Pegasus bridge on D-Day. This bridge crossed the Caen Canal. On June 6, troops secured this bridge and the Orne River bridge to stop advancing Germans.

Turn the page.

There's something sitting on the monument. It's a dented military helmet. You pick it up. It looks like a helmet worn by Allied paratroopers.

You head back to Omaha Beach. Maybe you can include the helmet in your exhibit! But in your excitement, it takes awhile for you to notice that the trail of blood has vanished.

THE END

To follow another path, turn to page 15.
To learn more about ghosts of war, turn to page 103.

You scurry into the telephone room and answer the ringing phone. Static and crackling come through the line. A voice on the other end shouts something in German. But you can't understand him. With a shaking hand, you hang up the phone.

The moment you let go of the phone, it vanishes. The bunker is empty. The German officers are gone, along with the table and maps. You're back in the present and ready to leave the ghosts of Pointe du Hoc. You'll question this experience for the rest of your life.

THE END

To follow another path, turn to page 15.
To learn more about ghosts of war, turn to page 103.

You frantically search the area for something to throw down to the man. A length of fraying rope lies in the grass. You scoop it up and hurry back to the edge. The man is now a few feet closer to the top.

"Hey!" you shout over the wind. "Do you want me to help pull you up?"

The man looks up. His uniform looks exactly like what the Army Rangers wore on D-Day. Brown jacket. Netting stretched over his helmet. But it can't be.

The man locks eyes with you. His face is pale, almost see-through. Your breath catches in your throat. Everything goes black. You tumble over the edge of the cliff at Pointe du Hoc.

When you open your eyes, you're tucked into the bed at your hotel. You have no bruises or scratches. Surely a fall from that height would have broken bones. It must have been a dream, you tell yourself. But you don't remember coming back to the hotel.

Maybe someone at the front desk remembers you coming back. You reach for your phone on the bedside table. But instead, you grab a piece of fraying rope.

THE END

To follow another path, turn to page 15.
To learn more about ghosts of war, turn to page 103.

You flee the beach and return to the small village on the bluff where you're staying. The moment your head hits the pillow, you fall into a deep sleep. You wake in the middle of the night after a terrible nightmare about D-Day.

German prisoners of war are fenced into an enclosure on Utah Beach on D-Day.

Unable to fall back asleep, you stumble out of bed and open the curtains. The streets and buildings look different. The cars are much older. The bakery is on fire. A few houses have been blown up. People scream and run. You can't believe your eyes! Terrified, you close the curtains.

You hide under the covers for a while before curiosity gets the better of you. This time when you open the curtains, the town is back to normal. You're baffled.

You're about to turn away when you notice a man limping down the street. He wears a military uniform, and he carries a gun. His uniform is greenish brown with a coat and baggy pants. He wears a pack on his back. You'd swear it was a British World War II uniform. You look for other soldiers, but he's the only one you see.

Turn the page.

He moves toward a brick building. You assume he's going to change directions. There are no doors on this side of the building. Instead, he passes right through it, as if it's made of air! You can't wait to tell Rebecca about this thrilling ghostly encounter at Normandy.

THE END

To follow another path, turn to page 15.
To learn more about ghosts of war, turn to page 103.

Ruins at the site of the Battle of Hastings

CHAPTER 5
THE GHOSTS OF WAR

Humans have waged war for thousands of years. The battlefields left behind are reminders of the violence that took place there. Some wars change the landscape forever. Fires and bullets destroy trees and greenery. Bombs level buildings and leave huge craters in the earth. Entire towns are wiped off the map. And the loss of human life is staggering.

In many ways, a battlefield is like a cemetery. In some battles, soldiers were buried where they fell. Often, the debris of war remains, such as used bullets and pieces of old uniforms. Odd sights and sounds at many battlefields lead some people to believe they're haunted by the dead.

Ghostly sightings at Battle Abbey didn't begin until the battlefield became a park in the 1970s. There are no documented firsthand accounts of a ghostly King Harold with an arrow stuck in his eye. So, where did the tale come from? The Bayeux Tapestry shows Harold shot through the eye with an arrow. Could the haunted story be rooted in truth?

The Battle of Gettysburg was the single bloodiest battle of the Civil War. Some of the earliest reported hauntings came from Iverson's Pits. They were located on the Forney farm.

This farm became a mass grave for Confederate soldiers after Alfred Iverson's failed attack. Farm workers were too afraid to work near the pits after sunset. Reports of ghostly activity at Gettysburg continue to the present day.

The Normandy invasion saw heavy losses for both the Allies and the Germans. On D-Day, historians estimate around 10,000 Allied soldiers were killed, wounded, or went missing. Soon after the war, stories of ghostly soldiers and the sound of gunfire became common in Normandy. People claim phantom tanks appear, only to vanish. The ghosts of paratroopers have been reported dangling from trees where they crashed. The spirits of dead soldiers have been spotted roaming the streets and beaches.

Are these ghostly battlefield tales true? Many visitors have had unsettling experiences at Hastings, Gettysburg, and Normandy. Does this mean these places are truly haunted? Or do these battlefields stir up such strong emotions that people experience things that aren't really there?

MORE GHOSTLY ENCOUNTERS

In 1990, Battle Abbey worker Daryl Burchmore was locking up the undercroft for the night. All the visitors were gone. He made sure all the rooms were empty. As soon as he locked the door, he heard shouting from inside the undercroft. "Let me out! Let me out!" a voice cried. When he unlocked the door, no one was there.

Devil's Den is one of the most-reported haunted spots at Gettysburg. Large boulders and crevices define the area. Fighting there was brutal. Many visitors have reported a ghostly soldier in tattered clothing wearing a floppy hat at Devil's Den.

On August 19, 1942, the Allies attempted to land on the coast of France at Dieppe. They stormed the beach around 5:00 a.m. But the mission failed. The Allies used what they learned at Dieppe to plan D-Day. In 1951, two sisters vacationing in Dieppe awoke to the sounds of war. They sat on their balcony and listened for three hours. The timing of the sounds they heard matched the records from the Dieppe invasion.

French citizens wave at American soldiers riding a tank through the rubble of a French town on D-Day.

OTHER PATHS TO EXPLORE

1. At Battle Abbey, tales of ghostly monks outnumber those of dead soldiers. The monks lived at the abbey for hundreds of years. Like English and Norman soldiers, many died there. But unlike the soldiers, their deaths were probably not violent. Why do you think so many people report seeing monks at the abbey?

2. If you were a park ranger at Gettysburg, would you believe the haunted tales? What would you do if you had a ghostly encounter of your own? Would you tell anyone about it? Do you think sensationalizing the hauntings dishonors those who died there?

3. Imagine visiting Omaha Beach in the present day. How would what you know about D-Day and the ghost stories affect your visit? Are you more or less likely to believe in ghosts after reading this book?

GLOSSARY

abbey (AB-ee)—a group of buildings where monks live and work

brigade (bri-GAYD)—a unit of an army

cosplayer (KAHZ-play-uhr)—someone who dresses up as famous historical or fictional characters

earl (UHRL)—a rich and powerful Englishman

electromagnetic field (i-lek-troh-mag-NET-ik FEELD)—a field of force created by moving electric charges

mace (MAYSS)—a type of club used as a weapon

paratrooper (PAIR-uh-troop-ur)—a soldier trained to jump by parachute into battle

replica (REP-luh-kuh)—an exact copy of something

retreat (ri-TREET)—to move back or withdraw from a difficult situation

secede (si-SEED)—to formally withdraw from a group or an organization, often to form another organization

BIBLIOGRAPHY

Beevor, Antony. *D-Day: The Battle for Normandy.* New York: Viking, 2009.

Coco, Gregory A. *A Strange and Blighted Land: Gettysburg: The Aftermath of a Battle.* Gettysburg, PA: Thomas Publications, 1995.

Marren, Peter. *1066: The Battles of York, Stamford Bridge & Hastings.* Barnsley, U.K.: Leo Cooper, 2004.

Nesbitt, Mark. *Ghosts of Gettysburg V: Spirits, Apparitions, and Haunted Places of the Battlefield.* Gettysburg, PA: Thomas Publications, 2000.

Pearse, Bowen. *Ghost-Hunter's Casebook: The Investigations of Andrew Green Revisited.* Stroud, Gloucestershire, United Kingdom: Tempus Publishing Group Limited, 2008.

Pfanz, Harry W. *Gettysburg: The First Day.* Chapel Hill, NC: University of North Carolina Press, 2010.

Swayne, Matthew. *Haunted World War II: Soldier Spirits, Ghost Planes & Strange Synchronicities.* Woodbury, MN: Llewellyn Publications, 2018.

READ MORE

Hubbard, Martha. *Gettysburg*. Lake Elmo, MN: Focus Readers, 2024.

Johnson, Jennifer. *Pickett's Charge at Gettysburg: A Bloody Clash in the Civil War*. New York: Scholastic, 2020.

Williams, Dinah. *Battlefield Ghosts: True Hauntings*. New York: Scholastic Press, an imprint of Scholastic Inc., 2021.

INTERNET SITES

American Battlefield Trust: Gettysburg
battlefields.org/learn/civil-war/battles/gettysburg

Daily Mail: The Ghosts of Normandy
dailymail.co.uk/news/article-9524833/The-ghosts-Normandy-Images-D-Day-landings-superimposed-modern-day-scenes.html

The Ghosts Of Normandy Past, In Sussex England
normandythenandnow.com/the-ghosts-of-normandy-past-in-sussex-england/

ABOUT THE AUTHOR

Megan Cooley Peterson is a children's book author and editor. When not writing, Megan enjoys movies, books, and all things Halloween. She lives in Minnesota with her husband and daughter.